AS & A LEVEL STUDY GUIDE FOR ANDREA LEVY'S *SMALL ISLAND* – STUDY GUIDE

(All chapters, page-by-page analysis)

by Joe Broadfoot
MA

Contents

INTRODUCTION

This book has been primarily written for students and teachers embarking on CIE's AS & A Level Literature in English (9695) Paper 3 Section B, which will be examined in 2020.

The idea behind this guide is to mostly point students and teachers towards language techniques used by the writer, which covers a lot of what is wanted by examiners in Assessment Objective 2 (AO2) and how form, structure and language shape meanings. The simple comprehension tasks and the higher-level questioning should ensure that all students are reading actively, while working primarily on the AO that many find the most challenging.

PROLOGUE (QUEENIE)

1. What's Queenie's teacher's nickname?
2. Who helps her mother with the pies?
3. Who feeds the pigs and the poultry?
4. What does her mother talk about with other butcher's wives?
5. What might it tell us about her parents?
6. Which part of the British Empire is most appealing to her?
7. What's Graham's attitude like to the African woman?
8. Who is portrayed as the most civilised?
9. How?
10. When is this part of the novel set?

Answers
1. Early Bird.
2. Inside girls.
3. Outside girls.
4. The bother of humane killing.
5. They're insensitive.
6. Australia.
7. Superior.
8. The African man.
9. Shaking hands, bowing, giving directions.
10. Between the wars.

ONE (HORTENSE)

1. Who is she thinking of at the start?
2. What seems to be going on between them?
3. Why does Hortense think the house is high-class, initially?
4. What does she lose?
5. What is her bag hyperbolically as big as?
6. What speed does her button travel at?
7. How is the white man pushing a trolley described?
8. In what ways does the taxi driver speak condescendingly to Hortense?
9. What simile is used to describe Gilbert's shirt?
10. Which Biblical figure is likened to Gilbert?
11. Why is that comparison ironic?
12. Although to Hortense, Gilbert's room is a prison, what is it to him?

Answers
1. Celia Langley.
2. Rivalry.
3. Pillars.
4. A button.
5. The Isle of Wight.
6. A bullet.
7. Picking his nose.
8. You got them (bells and knockers) where you come from?
9. Like a mischievous schoolboy's.
10. Moses.
11. This is not the promised land.
12. A palace.

TWO (GILBERT)

1. What does he claim to have living inside him?
2. What kind of circus act do Gilbert and Kenneth resemble?
3. How is Gilbert described upon reaching the top?
4. How does Hortense rub her case?
5. What does she focus on inside the room?
6. What happens to her white gloves?
7. What simile describes her gaping mouth?
8. What is the brush in Jean's hair described as?
9. How is Hortense's jump described?
10. What names does Gilbert finally call her?

Answer
1. An honourable man.
2. Pantomime clowns.
3. A wheezing old crone.
4. Like he bruised it.
5. A crack in the ceiling.
6. They go black.
7. Like a simpleton.
8. Like a hatchet.
9. Like a flea.
10. Little Miss High-class & Stick-up-your-nose-in-the-air.

THREE (HORTENSE)

1. Write down three attributes of her father, who is a man of _____, _____ and _____.
2. Who is Alberta?
3. How is Alberta described in comparison to Lovell Roberts?
4. What does this reveal about Hortense?
5. How does Mr Philip Roberts's sense of responsibility and authority manifest itself physically?
6. What relation is Miss Jewel to Hortense?
7. What simile describes how Michael Roberts puffs out his chest?
8. What simile describes how Mr Philip Roberts clutches his Bible?
9. What happens to the 'perfumed water'?
10. Where does Hortense think God was born?
11. What does Mr Philip Roberts think about evangelists?
12. Why?
13. What colour imagery is used to describe Mr Ryder's head?
14. What three attributes does Michael have?
15. Who does he remind you of?
16. Does Michael believe in teachings from the Bible?
17. What quotation backs that up?
18. Which Shakespearean play is referred to?
19. How is Mr Philip Roberts's face described?
20. What does Mrs Roberts glow like, after Michael's comment?
21. How does Hortense discover that Michael knows Mrs Ryder intimately?
22. What flies into the room?
23. What simile describes Mr Ryder?
24. Which animal is Miss Ma likened to?
25. What next flies in on the breeze?
26. What qualities does Miss Ma think the men of the RAF and her son possess?

Answers
1. Class, character, intelligence.
2. Hortense's mother.

3. Inferior.
4. She's proud of her father, but not her mother.
5. Through 'two fleshy jowls'.
6. Maternal grandmother.
7. Like a cock.
8. Like a weapon.
9. It falls to the earth.
10. England.
11. He doesn't like them.
12. He thinks they froth at the mouth like beasts.
13. Red as a berry.
14. Class, character, intelligence.
15. Hortense's father.
16. No.
17. Descended from monkeys.
18. *Romeo and Juliet*.
19. Like a stone.
20. Like a lantern.
21. He calls Mrs Ryder, 'Stella'.
22. A dead cloth shoe.
23. Like a piece of cloth.
24. A snake.
25. Rumours.
26. Courage and good breeding.

FOUR (HORTENSE)

1. What does she complain of in her hind region?
2. What does it tell us about her character?
3. What are the dazzling girls compared to?
4. What simile is used to describe Miss Morgan's smile?
5. In Hortense's dream, what is Michael portrayed holding in his hand?
6. What might it tell us about Michael's character?
7. Which Biblical character is the girl in the dream compared to?
8. Why?
9. Who was it that pulled Hortense from her bed?
10. Which Shakespearean play is alluded to?
11. Which other Biblical characters are mentioned?
12. What is Celia described as being like?
13. What alliterative tricolon is used to describe the soldiers?
14. What simile describes the woman, who accosts Franklin?
15. What is the truth about the woman's hair?
16. What simile is used to show how Celia's mother points out the airman?
17. Who does Hortense blame for being led from the path of righteousness?
18. What is strange about Miss Morgan's eyes?
19. What does Miss Morgan think about true grief?
20. What is trembling in Hortense's hands?

Answers
1. Paralysis.
2. She exaggerates her complaints.
3. Butterflies.
4. Like the leer of a church gargoyle.
5. A scorpion.
6. Reckless, irresponsible, risk-taker.
7. Eve.
8. It's about succumbing to temptation.
9. Celia Langley.
10. Henry V.
11. Solomon and Job.
12. A flower.

13. Dashing, daring and daft.
14. Like a child.
15. It's a wig.
16. Like a dress.
17. Celia.
18. They are not the same colour.
19. It is silent.
20. Foreboding.

FIVE (HORTENSE)

1. Which simile describes the sense of connection she feels towards Michael?
2. Does it suggest a strong or weak connection?
3. What simile conveys how she is enclosed by another man?
4. How could this be significant?
5. What is the man in the habit of doing?
6. What simile is used to describe Michael's imaginary return?
7. What does it suggest?

Answers
1. Like a thread.
2. Weak as barely discernible, although it could be deceptively strong.
3. Firm as a knot.
4. Perhaps she will tie the knot (get married) with him (foreshadowing).
5. Smiling and laughing at his own jokes.
6. Like a pinpoint of light on a cave wall.
7. Michael is almost divine and very civilised compared to the cavemen.

SIX (HORTENSE)

1. Write down a phrase that reveals her idealism.
2. Write down a phrase that sums up her attitude towards the Andersons.
3. What advice does Celia give Hortense?
4. How does Celia describe her man, using a simile?
5. Who does the man remind Hortense of, when he laughs?
6. What does he (Gilbert) look like he bought when he's walking with Celia and Hortense?
7. What does he compare the Houses of Parliament to?
8. How does Hortense extinguish the light in Celia's eyes?
9. How does Celia react?

Answers
1. My dream was [...] to drink from the fountain of the English curriculum.
2. I puzzled on the need for both of them [Rosa's grandsons] to exist.
3. Take your time to get to know the Andersons.
4. Charming as a prince.
5. Michael.
6. The moon and the stars.
7. A fairytale castle.
8. By telling Gilbert that Celia's mother is insane.
9. She punches Hortense.

SEVEN (HORTENSE)

1. What simile describes how Gilbert nods?
2. Who does Gilbert think Michael is?
3. Where does Gilbert get money for the trip from?
4. What flower imagery illustrates Hortense's naivety?
5. Which word is personified, as Hortense imagines how she will rise higher socially than the company she now keeps.
6. Which line shows how honest Gilbert is, despite his earlier white lies.
7. Which Biblical simile is used to describe Gilbert, after Hortense takes off her hat.
8. Which animal is Gilbert compared to, as he hops around?

Answers
1. Like a half-wit.
2. Hortense's brother.
3. Hortense lends it to him (she's been prudent financially).
4. Daffodils, which are mostly pale and not all colours of the rainbow, like she imagines.
5. Disdain.
6. You have me there.
7. Naked as Adam.
8. A jackass.

EIGHT (HORTENSE)

1. Why does Hortense feel justified in looking down her nose at the landlady?
2. How might the 'war blanket' be symbolic?

Answers
1. Because she makes money from renting out rooms.
2. It shows how love takes years and cannot be rushed, like the sewing of the blanket, thread by thread (see Michael).

NINE (QUEENIE)

1. What tricolon does the writer use to show Mr Todd's emotional response towards immigration?
2. How does the writer illustrate Mr Todd's attitude towards Jean?
3. How does the writer create mystery?
4. Why are Mrs Blanche Smith's daughters scared of their father?
5. According to Mr Morris Smith, what makes black people dangerous?
6. What does Blanche equate immigration to?
7. What does Morris expect black people to do if I white person is walking in the same street?

Answers
1. Outrage, shock, fear.
2. He choked on his cup of tea.
3. We're not told exactly about the 'incident' involving Gilbert, so we can only guess.
4. He's become a stranger to them.
5. Animal desires.
6. Hitler invading.
7. Get out of the way.

TEN (HORTENSE)

1. Why does she think Gilbert can't be trusted?
2. What bird imagery describes how she remembers Gilbert in Jamaica?
3. What does she imagine the mice are doing?

Answers
1. She catches his 'greedy eye' perusing her.
2. Puffed as a peacock.
3. Pushing a piano, wearing boots.

ELEVEN (GILBERT)

1. Which simile describes how Gilbert regards himself in uniform?
2. Why does he think 'America is Paradise' initially?
3. After eating, what do the men's thoughts return to?
4. Where does his Jewish father metaphorically meet Jesus?
5. Why was Gilbert's brother, Lester, rejected by the RAF?
6. What is Gilbert ready to fight?
7. Which words hit the men 'like an explosion'?

Answers
1. Like a god.
2. The food quality.
3. Women.
4. On the battlefield.
5. Not white, not of pure English descent.
6. The master race theory.
7. No white women will consort with them, when they get to England.

TWELVE (GILBERT)

1. What animal imagery describes how volunteers huddle together?
2. What does Thwaites think of the volunteers?
3. Why is the dog and gecko story relevant?
4. What simile describes how the locals get to know the volunteers?
5. Which three words describe England, in reality?
6. Name three beautiful things in Jamaica, which are missed.
7. What three things do English people expect to find in Jamaica?
8. What effect does the blindfold analogy create?

Answers
1. Nesting birds
2. All thoroughly stupid.
3. Because the volunteers are like the gecko, while the fascinated villagers are similar to the dog.
4. Like a chink in a dam?
5. Ragged, old and dirty.
6. Cockpit county, pink hibiscus and Dunn's river.
7. Savages, jungles and swinging through trees.
8. Gilbert is disorientated and disillusioned, but perhaps still blind to the faults of the Mother Country.

THIRTEEN (GILBERT)

1. What is the sergeant puzzling about?
2. How does Gilbert feel behind a wheel?
3. What role does Gilbert expect in the RAF?
4. What role is he assigned?

Answers
1. Whether all darkies are daft.
2. A frustrated prisoner.
3. A wireless operator, air-gunner or flight engineer.
4. Driver.

FOURTEEN (GILBERT)

1. What falls from his hair, when he bows?
2. What is blame compared to?
3. To what, does Gilbert attribute his politeness?
4. How are the officer's teeth described?
5. How does Gilbert feel when food is brought out?
6. What is the coffee compared to?
7. How does Jon sit?
8. What is the changeability of the military compared to?
9. A black man at an American base is as welcome as what?
10. Which area is reserved for black GIs?
11. Who is described as a puppet master?
12. How does Jon move on his seat?
13. Where are Job and Levy dropped off?

Answers
1. A light rain of soot.
2. Bullets in a battle.
3. Mother-bred instinct.
4. Standing to attention.
5. Like a dignatory.
6. Water lapping on a shore.
7. Like an idle puppet.
8. A summer breeze.
9. A snake in a crib.
10. Nottingham.
11. Jon.
12. Twitching tormentedly.
13. The middle of nowhere.

FIFTEEN (GILBERT)

1. How does the writer link love, death and decay?
2. Why?
3. What is a Lancaster?
4. What does the man's face contort into?
5. How does Gilbert speak to the man?
6. What simile describes Queenie Bligh?
7. What simile describes how Arthur would be flattened by Paul Robeson?
8. What does Gilbert say is part of his war effort?

Answers
1. Gilbert is portrayed as sitting on a bench for lovers, going through a rotten (decaying) cemetery (death) fate.
2. To show new love can spring up when old love slowly dies.
3. A bomber.
4. A soundless scream.
5. As if he were talking to a child.
6. As pretty as a doll.
7. Like a hut before a tank.
8. Laughter.

SIXTEEN (GILBERT)

1. What simile is used to describe a white GI?
2. What simile is used to describe Queenie's silhouette of her legs?
3. How does the writer use alliteration to show the animated nature of Queenie's laugh?
4. What simile is used to describe three white GIs in the tea shop?
5. The GIs concentrate on Gilbert and Queenie like they are what?
6. What sound imagery and simile is used to convey the GIs' frustration?
7. How is Gilbert viewed by the GIs, as the watch him through the window?

Answers
1. Like a silly schoolgirl.
2. Like a saucy picture show.
3. It 'filled every of the dull and door room with dazzle.
4. Like snipers clearing their aim.
5. An exam they must pass.
6. Snorting like beasts.
7. As if vermin were escaping.

SEVENTEEN (GILBERT)

1. What is described as the mental equal of the GIs in the tea shop?
2. What does the usherette flick in Gilbert's face?
3. What are the black GIs described as?
4. What simile describes the silhouette of the GI, who first stands up?
5. What historical battle is mentioned?
6. What simile is used to describe the manager's arms?
7. What simile describes the usherette's disappearance?
8. What oxymoron describes the clash?
9. What simile describes how a stomach feels when punched?
10. Who becomes another casualty of war?

Answers
1. Cattle.
2. The torchlight.
3. Writhing cockroaches.
4. A mortal tempest.
5. Waterloo.
6. Waving like a drowning man.
7. Like a laxative.
8. A venomous ballet.
9. Like a cushion.
10. Arthur.

EIGHTEEN (GILBERT)

1. What simile is used to describe the boys jumping into the sea?
2. What does this remind the reader?
3. What mistake do the press make when writing about Queenie?
4. How does Gilbert feel about being demobilised?
5. Who is Elwood's mother?
6. Who is credited with giving Jamaicans the vote?
7. What metaphorical verb describes what happens to money?
8. What alliterative simile describes Elwood exerting himself?
9. Which simile describing Elwood works as a foreshadowing device regarding Gilbert's future?
10. Which flying bomb are the bees compared to?
11. Which simile describes Enid?
12. What is left in the jars?
13. According to Elwood, what must Jamaica get rid of?
14. Why does Elwood think Gilbert wants to return to England?
15. Why does it seem that Hortense wants to marry Gilbert?

Answers
1. Like an explosion of starfish.
2. Gilbert has returned from explosions during the war as a kind of star.
3. They think she's Arthur's daughter.
4. Quizzical as a jilted lover.
5. Auntie Corinne.
6. Norman Manley.
7. Flying.
8. Sturdy as a stallion.
9. Veiled as a bride.
10. A doodlebug.
11. Furry as a grisly bear.
12. Sunlight.
13. The white man.
14. His father's white.
15. To escape Jamaica and go to England.

NINETEEN (GILBERT)

1. What colour is the sunshine in England?
2. What does the 'brooch' end up as?
3. Which theme does it link to?
4. What is the 'quiet horror' of landlords and landladies compared to?
5. What is personified as troubling Gilbert's hand, as he rings the bell?

Answers
1. Grey.
2. A cluster of flies.
3. Beguiling illusions.
4. Like a cloud before the sun.
5. Trepidation.

TWENTY (HORTENSE)

1. What alarms her about her first morning in England?
2. What does she feel towards Gilbert?

Answers
1. Rudely awoken, steam, the cold, the dark.
2. Sorrow.

TWENTY–ONE (GILBERT)

1. To not be heard by Queenie, what does Gilbert need to do?
2. What does he compare finding Queenie to?
3. What does he become skilled at?

Answers
1. Float down.
2. Sipping rum punch from a golden bowl.
3. Lying.

TWENTY-TWO (HORTENSE)

1. What does she imagine she can hear?
2. Which idiom confuses Hortense?
3. What does Hortense think Queenie means by using that idiom?
4. What does Queenie think Hortense will need to look at the blanket?
5. When Queenie discovers that Gilbert hadn't mentioned her to Hortense, how does she feel?
6. What information does Hortense want?

Answers
1. Celia laughing.
2. Cat got your tongue?
3. She's lost her cat.
4. Dark glasses.
5. As if stabbed.
6. How to make a chip.

TWENTY-THREE (QUEENIE)

1. How are her mother's hands described?
2. What is her father's hair cursed by?
3. How are the boys and girls described?
4. What does it suggest about Queenie?
5. What does her father receive?
6. What does it mean?
7. What does her mother call all the girls?
8. What does Little Jim catch?
9. Who is Early Bird?
10. What does Queenie imagine that other girls admire in mirrors?
11. Where do Wilfred's teeth point?
12. What does Queenie think her father will do to Harry?
13. Who promises to 'better' Queenie?

Answers
1. Hands that clasp like a vice, arms as strong as a bear's.
2. A 'cow's lick'.
3. Stupid and dozy.
4. Condescending, superior attitude.
5. A white feather.
6. Cowardice.
7. Girl.
8. Rheumatic fever.
9. Miss Earl.
10. Their Cupid's-bow mouths.
11. Any direction but down.
12. Kill him.
13. Aunt Dorothy.

TWENTY–FOUR (QUEENIE)

1. What's the name of Queenie's elocution teacher?
2. What simile describes Prudence, the poodle?
3. What is Prudence's growl compared to?
4. What does Dorothy associate Cockneys with?
5. What does Bernard's vein look like?
6. What is kissing him compared to?
7. In Dorothy's dialogue, what metaphor is used to describe Bernard.
8. What does Dorothy fall on?
9. Why did Montgomery never have a problem lifting Dorothy?

Answers
1. Mrs Waterfall.
2. Like a posh privet hedge.
3. As terrifying as an old man clearing his throat.
4. Jellied eels and knees-ups.
5. A worm.
6. Kissing a chicken's beak.
7. A brick.
8. Prudence.
9. Because she was his duchess.

TWENTY–FIVE (QUEENIE)

1. What colours does Bernard go, when he holds his breath?
2. What alliterative phrase describes how Queenie's face looks with powder on?
3. What simile describes how Bernard and his father live?

Answers
1. Pink.
2. Porcelain perfection.
3. Like a couple of unwelcome mice.

TWENTY-SIX (QUEENIE)

1. Whose speech does Queenie nearly miss?
2. What language is 'schnell'?
3. What is the shelter described as?
4. What happens to Mr Plant?
5. What's an 'ack-ack'?
6. What is homeless woman's face as unreadable as?
7. What is the child's toy horse made of?
8. How is melody of a dropping bomb described?
9. What does number thirty look like?
10. What does Queenie think about the phrase: 'Safe as houses'?
11. What is found in number thirty?
12. What does Bernard say, when refusing to house the homeless family?

Answers
1. Chamberlain's.
2. German.
3. A tunnel.
4. He's interned.
5. Anti-aircraft gunfire.
6. A corpse.
7. A sock.
8. A sharp descending note.
9. A skull.
10. Even solid can crumble.
11. A brooch.
12. He says: 'They're not our sort'.

TWENTY-SEVEN (QUEENIE)

1. Which simile describes how smouldering survivors of a bomb attack look?
2. What does it highlight about World War Two?
3. Why do some giggle after losing everything?
4. What is an Anderson?
5. When do the War Damage Commission pay out?
6. What is the road to hell paved with?
7. How is Bernard's vein described, when Queenie gives away furniture?
8. What does Queenie regret saying to Bernard?

Answers
1. Like a burnt pie.
2. It was fought on the domestic front too.
3. Hysterical euphoria.
4. A bomb shelter.
5. After the war.
6. Good intentions.
7. Pumping like it had a heart of its own.
8. 'There's thousand [...] having much more of a war than you are'.

TWENTY-EIGHT (QUEENIE)

1. How does the back of Bernard's neck look now?
2. What type of punctuation describes Arthur?
3. What metaphor describes how much Queenie appreciates Arthur?
4. Who are the three RAF officers she meets at her house?
5. How is Michael's smile described?
6. What does Queenie do for the first time in a long while?
7. What are Michael's lively eyes compared to?
8. What did Queenie think Michael's moustache was initially?
9. What is Michael the colour of?
10. How can this be appropriate?
11. Where does Queenie think Jamaica is?
12. What does Michael claim to see in the midst of the devastated city?

Answers
1. Fearless.
2. A human apostrophe.
3. A magician.
4. Ginger, Kip and Sergeant Michael Roberts.
5. Picture-house.
6. Takes care of her appearance.
7. Fairy lights.
8. A black shadow.
9. A conker.
10. Because conkers are used for battling and they involve physical contact.
11. Africa.
12. A hummingbird.

TWENTY-NINE (QUEENIE)

1. How is Queenie described, using silibance?
2. How is Arthur's reticence describes theatrically?
3. What does Queenie swear someone was doing?
4. Which simile describes how Queenie is smouldering?
5. What does Queenie step on?
6. How could it be symbolic?
7. Which simile describes Arthur's new-found stability?
8. What does Arthur do for the first time in front of Queenie, that is particularly shocking?

Answers
1. Sexy as any starlet on a silver screen.
2. A blank curtain.
3. Taking her photograph.
4. Like a kipper.
5. A severed hand with a ring on it.
6. She's disrespecting her marriage by having an affair.
7. Steady as a rock.
8. He speaks.

THIRTY (GILBERT)

1. What one word describes Gilbert?
2. What simile describes how the office workers look at him?
3. How often does the foreman use his name?
4. What simile describes how much Gilbert yearns for home?
5. What simile describes the Post Office workers at King's Cross?
6. What simile describes how pitifully Gilbert feels?
7. What does Gilbert insist that Hortense never does?

Answers
1. Driver.
2. Watching me close as a pickpocket.
3. Once.
4. As a drunk man for whiskey.
5. As idle as layabouts.
6. As a whipped dog.
7. Go down on her knees.

THIRTY-ONE (HORTENSE)

1. Metaphorically, what can Hortense do with Gilbert's bottom lip?
2. Which simile describes how Gilbert blocks the heat?
3. What simile describes how Hortense must crawl?
4. Which simile describes the steam rising from Gilbert's coat?

Answers
1. Wipe a postage stamp on it.
2. As a stormcloud before the sun.
3. Like a cringing dog.
4. Like a dragon.

THIRTY-TWO (GILBERT)

1. Which simile describes how the rain strikes him?
2. What is personified with its hand clasped to Gilbert's throat?
3. What is the candy described as?
4. How does Hortense pop the chip into her mouth?

Answers
1. Cold as steel pins.
2. Regret.
3. Precious.
4. Greedy. (Greedily)

THIRTY-THREE (HORTENSE)

1. What is Queenie wrapped in?
2. What has the Almighty 'stolen'?
3. What is the miscomprehension between Hortense and Queenie described as?
4. What kind of teacher is Queenie?
5. What rude names is Hortense called?
6. What drains the pink from Queenie's face?

Answers
1. A dowdy woollen coat.
2. The rainbow.
3. A silly dance.
4. A punctilious one.
5. Golliwog and sambo.
6. The sight of Bernard.

THIRTY-FOUR (QUEENIE)

1. What does she want from Bernard?

Answer
1. An explanation.

THIRTY-FIVE (BERNARD)

1. How were they packed onto the train?
2. What are the cakes speckled with?
3. What is 'India's spell' changed to?
4. Who does Queenie think Bernard wants to be like?
5. What does the Japanese gunfire ping and pop like?
6. What simile describes the Hurricanes after the attack?
7. What does Maxi's calloused hand feel like?
8. What do the Gurkhas do with the Japanese POW?

Answers
1. Like cattle.
2. Flies.
3. India's smell.
4. Biggles.
5. Harmless fireworks.
6. Like colanders.
7. Knotted wood.
8. Kill him.

THIRTY-SIX (BERNARD)

1. What has war done to his back and step?
2. What kind of toys are Japanese soldiers, according to Bernard?
3. How Bernard's colour described?
4. What simile describes Maxi attacking the fake snake?
5. What is Bernard dreaming of?
6. What are Bernard and Maxi's eyes alert as?
7. What is the shared blanket metaphorically referred to as?
8. What do the letters RSU stand for?
9. What simile describes Maxi's fear?

Answers
1. Put a rod in his back and a spring in his step.
2. Clockwork,
3. Molten and brown as a warm bar if chocolate.
4. Like Tarzan.
5. Snow.
6. Prey.
7. The cocoon.
8. Repair and Salvage Unit.
9. Bloodless as a corpse.

THIRTY–SEVEN (BERNARD)

1. What simile describes Queenie's hair?
2. What do you need to hold an enema for seven hours.
3. What simile describes a POW's bones jangling?
4. Which word is repeated three times in close succession?
5. Where is Bernard sent to?

Answers
1. Obedient as thread.
2. Iron will and stamina of a bull.
3. Like coins in a bag.
4. Forgotten.
5. Calcutta.

THIRTY-EIGHT (BERNARD)

1. What simile describes the ash?
2. What simile describes the stench?
3. What does the NCO look like?
4. What is the corpse as stiff as?
5. What simile describes how they are surrounded?

Answers
1. Like tropical snow.
2. Sharp as toothache.
3. Varnished and blood-vessel red.
4. An ironing board.
5. As water.

THIRTY-NINE (BERNARD)

1. What alliterative phrase describes what only British troops could do?
2. What simile describes Pierpoint's arms?
3. What simile describes Queenie's buttons?
4. What does Bernard think the British Empire represents?
5. What simile describes how chaotic the meeting becomes?

Answers
1. Keep those coolies under control.
2. As long as an ape's.
3. Like padlocks.
4. Decency.
5. Like a classroom with the teacher gone.

FORTY (BERNARD)

1. What do they patch up a kite's cloth bodywork with?
2. What did a priest lose?
3. What does Bernard dislike about India?
4. Who is the famous war-time singer referred to?
5. What is King George VI's stutter described as being like?
6. What famous soap product is mentioned?
7. What simile describes how Bernard was frothing.

Answers
1. A chap's shirt.
2. His entire church.
3. Heat and mosquitoes.
4. Vera Lynn.
5. A devil is holding back his tongue.
6. Lifebuoy.
7. Like a sponge.

FORTY-ONE (BERNARD)

1. How are Bernard's eyelids described?
2. Which simile describes the fire engine?
3. Which simile describes how the 'coolie' backs away?
4. Which simile describes how the 'coolie' is less than a man to Bernard.

Answers
1. Like barbed wire.
2. Slow as molasses.
3. Like a cringing dog.
4. Cowering like a girl.

FORTY-TWO (BERNARD)

1. What is the name of the Flight Lieutenant?
2. How is his skin described?
3. What's the punishment for losing a rifle?
4. What does the officer think was happening in the basha?
5. What makes the officer's stammer disappear?

Answers
1. Moon.
2. Rashed as pink as bully beef.
3. Court martial.
4. A meeting.
5. Anger.

FORTY-THREE (BERNARD)

1. Which simile describes the surface Bernard sleeps on?
2. What simile describes it when it gets wet?
3. What is Bernard's father given by a young girl?
4. How many years does Bernard's mother age in ten years?
5. Which simile describes Queenie's lack of passion for Bernard?
6. What do the words: 'Dear Queenie' turn into?

Answers
1. Hard as a biscuit ration.
2. Soggy as a biscuit dunked in tea.
3. A white feather.
4. Sixty.
5. Like a limp rag.
6. A blot.

FORTY-FOUR (BERNARD)

1. How does the CO tell Bernard that he's been demobilised?
2. How are the vultures described?
3. What is Johnny Pierpoint's winking eye like?
4. What shape do Pierpoint's eyebrows make?
5. What school simile describes Bernard's physical struggle with Pierpoint.
6. How is the girl's wiggling described?
7. What simile describes the effect of her tenderness?

Answers
1. Like he'd won it in a raffle.
2. Like scrawny hunch-backed hags.
3. A faulty bulb.
4. A hooded V.
5. Like a dunce with a bully.
6. Like a blasted dancer in a bazaar.
7. Shocking as a bolt from a current.

FORTY–FIVE (BERNARD)

1. What does transportation look like compared to the Wellington bomber?
2. Where does Bernard sleep?
3. What simile describes the ulcer's presence?
4. What does Bernard imagine Queenie doing?

Answers
1. Puny as tin toys.
2. In a lifeboat.
3. Like a galloping pulse.
4. Untying her apron.

FORTY-SIX (BERNARD)

1. How does Queenie react to seeing Bernard?
2. What is the longing for something familiar compared to?
3. How does Bernard feel seeing Maxi's son?
4. What does WR stand for?
5. What does Queenie think Bernard was doing in Brighton?
6. What were bones in Queenie's neck standing out like?
7. How are Gilbert's eyes described?

Answers
1. She's appalled.
2. Hunger.
3. Like a thief.
4. Wassermann Reaction.
5. Having a holiday.
6. Scaffolding.
7. Popping out.

FORTY-SEVEN (QUEENIE)

1. What does she see in the mirror?
2. Which film stars are mentioned?
3. How is a potential kiss from Bernard described?
4. In what way does Bernard move into the kitchen?
5. What was Queenie's toast like?
6. What might sand symbolise?
7. What does Queenie feel in Bernard's presence?

Answers
1. Hundreds of terrified Queenies.
2. Clark Gable and Vivien Leigh.
3. A peck from the chicken's beak.
4. Skipped.
5. Sandpaper.
6. Time.
7. Smothered.

FORTY-EIGHT (BERNARD)

1. What kind of plane does he dream about?
2. What does Queenie say to the pilot in Bernard's dream?
3. Why is that significant?

Answers
1. A Zero.
2. Hello. Come in.
3. He imagines she has invited someone he regards as the enemy into his house.

FORTY-NINE (GILBERT)

1. How is Hortense's back described?
2. What does Kenneth metaphorically throw off?
3. What does Gilbert have to explain about tax?
4. What metaphorically takes residence in Gilbert's boots?
5. How is Hortense's scowl described?
6. What word repeats in Hortense's dialogue, when she expresses her opinion of Kenneth?
7. What kind of creature does this make Hortense?

Answers
1. Folded like a crone's.
2. Hortense's ferocious look.
3. Everyone pays it.
4. His heart.
5. One bitter lemon.
6. Uncouth.
7. Insufferable.

FIFTY (HORTENSE)

1. What metaphorically slips from Gilbert's face and bumps on the floor.
2. What does Hortense think of a Cockney accent?
3. What is Gilbert grinning like?
4. What is Seymour's face covered with?
5. Which word is repeated in the receptionist's dialogue?
6. What is the receptionist's stale smile compared to?
7. When leaving, where does Hortense find herself?

Answers
1. His silly carefree countenance.
2. A low class slurring garble.
3. A buffoon.
4. Raw pimples and pustules.
5. Where?
6. A gargoyle's.
7. In a closet/cupboard.

FIFTY-ONE (GILBERT)

1. How does Gilbert follow Hortense?
2. What animal name describes how Gilbert thinks Hortense is as a wife.
3. According to Charlie Denton, what did Wellington win?
4. What is wrong with that?
5. How does Hortense blow her nose?
6. According to Gilbert, one thaw is not a what?
7. How reverent is Hortense when sightseeing?
8. What is Hortense's mood compared to?
9. What technique is this?
10. What is Gilbert's hopeless dream?
11. How does Hortense describe England?

Answers
1. Like a lame dog.
2. A wretched shrew.
3. The battle of Trafalgar Square.
4. Square is wrong.
5. With the force of a hurricane.
6. Summer.
7. As the devout before an altar.
8. Dark cold fog.
9. Pathetic fallacy.
10. He will study 'the law'.
11. Very cold.

FIFTY-TWO (BERNARD)

1. How does Bernard feel going into Gilbert's room?
2. What does Bernard think of colonial types?
3. What has the damp done to Gilbert and Hortense?
4. What are Gilbert's eyes bulging like?
5. What is Queenie puffing like?
6. What is Queenie's face blushing like?
7. How do Queenie and Hortense stagger out?

Answers
1. Like a thief.
2. Cunning.
3. Made them drop and sag.
4. A savage's.
5. A bulldog.
6. A raspberry ripple.
7. Like battle casualties.

FIFTY-THREE (HORTENSE)

1. Why is Hortense worried about locking the door?
2. What does Hortense think is under the bandage?
3. Which film is alluded to?
4. A tricolon describes the room as what?
5. Which sibilant tricolon is used to describe Queenie's actions?
6. What simile is used to describe how Queenie watches Hortense tying knots?
7. What religious simile is used to describe Queenie?

Answers
1. She's afraid of being incarcerated with this writhing woman.
2. An oozing gash or pus-y idents of a vicious bite.
3. *Gone With The Wind*.
4. Malodorous, stale and airless.
5. Straining, squeezing, and screaming.
6. Strict as a teacher.
7. Serene as a Madonna.

FIFTY-FOUR (GILBERT)

1. Which oxymoron effectively illustrates confusion?
2. How is Bernard's anger conveyed in Biblical terms?
3. How does Bernard deflate?
4. What simile describes Jean?
5. How are Hortense's white gloves described?
6. What simile describes what Hortense does with her head?

Answers
1. Noisy quiet.
2. Wrath of Samson.
3. Fast as a pricked balloon.
4. Powdered and painted as an ugly doll.
5. Like two fireflies in the dark.
6. She burrows it in Gilbert's neck like a chastened child.

FIFTY-FIVE (QUEENIE)

1. What can some words do once spoken?
2. What alliterative simile describes Michael?
3. How does Michael hold his lucky charm?
4. Which line is evidence of Queenie's elocution lessons?
5. Which tricolon shows Mr Todd and his sister in a negative light?
6. Does Bernard look at Queenie when she explains what has happened?

Answers
1. Split the world in two.
2. Casual as a cowboy.
3. Reverent as a Bible.
4. In Herefordshire, Hertfordshire and Hampshire hurricanes hardly ever happen.
5. Nudging, pointing, whispering.
6. No.

FIFTY-SIX (GILBERT)

1. Where does his tongue go when he hears a business proposition?
2. What does Winston have on the back of his hand?
3. What military metaphor describes Winston arriving at the right time?
4. How does Gilbert show his romantic side?
5. What does Hortense do with her arms?
6. Which simile conveys how crumpled Gilbert has been?
7. How does Hortense close the blanket over Gilbert?

Answers
1. In his cheek.
2. Two freckles.
3. Cavalry.
4. He buys flowers.
5. She throws out her arms wide.
6. As a moth from its cocoon.
7. As efficient as a mother.

FIFTY–SEVEN (BERNARD)

1. What comfort does Bernard get from the house?
2. What is Bernard as blank as?
3. What happens to his finger?
4. What does he apologise for?

Answers
1. Familiar four walls.
2. A sheet of white paper.
3. It's sucked by the baby like it was nectar.
4. Not being a better husband.

FIFTY-EIGHT (QUEENIE)

1. What did all the fighting men want?
2. What do Bernard and Gilbert look like they're about to do again?
3. When Bernard leaves the room what is it like?
4. When it comes to Michael, what are Queenie's ears like?
5. What does Hortense say happened to her brother, Michael?
6. Is it true?
7. What happens to the milk?
8. What symbolic meaning could it have?
9. What colour does the angry Bernard go?
10. How does Bernard want to explain Michael to the neighbours?
11. Where does Queenie want Michael to be?

Answers
1. A new start.
2. Lock horns.
3. The sun coming out.
4. Keen as a bat's.
5. Killed in the war.
6. No. Michael is her cousin and he wasn't killed in the war.
7. It spills.
8. No use crying over spilt milk.
9. Red as a berry.
10. Adopted.
11. With his own kind.

FIFTY-NINE (HORTENSE)

1. What adjective describes how Hortense feels about Queenie's actions?
2. What rude name is Gilbert called by Bernard, after: 'How dare you?'
3. What does Bernard say after Gilbert's impressive speech?
4. Why have Jamaicans always thought Hortense's future is golden?
5. What does Hortense think Michael will do one day?
6. What does Hortense do with what she finds?

Answers
1. Preposterous.
2. Savage.
3. I just can't understand.
4. Because of her golden skin.
5. Torment spiders, dress up a cat, look at a bird's nest.
6. Keeps it secret.

ESSAY PLANNING

In order to write a good essay, it is necessary to plan. In fact, it is best to quite formulaic in an exam situation, as you won't have much time to get started. Therefore, I will ask you to learn the following acronym: **DATMC (Definition, Application, Terminology, Main, Conclusion**. Some schools call it: **GSLMC (General, Specific, Link, Main, Conclusion)**, but it amounts to the same thing. The first three letters concern the introduction. (Of course, the alternative is to leave some blank lines and write your introduction after you have completed the main body of your essay, but it is probably not advisable for most students).

Let us first look at the following exam question, which is on poetry (of course, the same essay-planning principles apply to essays on novels and plays as well).

QUESTION: Explore how the poet conveys **feelings** in the poem.

STEP ONE: Identify the **keyword** in the question. (I have already done this, by highlighting it in **bold**). If you are following GSLMC, you now need to make a **general statement** about what feelings are. Alternatively, if you're following DATMC, simply **define** 'feelings'. For example, 'Feelings are emotional states or reactions or vague, irrational ideas and beliefs'.

STEP TWO: If you are following GSLMC, you now need to make a **specific statement** linking feelings (or whatever else you've defined) to how they appear in the poem. Alternatively, if you're following DATMC, simply define which 'feelings' **apply** in this poem. For example, 'The feelings love, fear and guilt appear in this poem, and are expressed by the speaker in varying degrees.'

STEP THREE: If you are following GSLMC, you now need to make a **link statement** identifying the methods used to convey the feelings (or whatever else you've defined) in the poem. Alternatively, if you're following DATMC, simply define which **techniques** are used to convey 'feelings' in this poem. For example, 'The poet primarily uses alliteration to emphasise his heightened emotional state, while hyperbole and enjambment also help to convey the sense that the speaker is descending into a state of madness.

STEP FOUR: Whether you are following GSLMC or DATMC, the next stage is more or less the same. The main part of the essay involves writing around **six paragraphs**, using whichever variation of PEEE you prefer. In my example, I will use **Point, Evidence, Exploration, Effect** on the listener. To make your essay even stronger, try to use your quotations chronologically. It will be easier for the examiner to follow, which means you are more likely to achieve a higher grade. To be more specific, I recommend that you take and analyse two quotations from the beginning of the poem, two from the middle, and two at the end.

STEP FIVE: Using Carol Ann Duffy's poem, 'Stealing', here's an example of how you could word one of your six paragraphs: **(POINT)** 'Near the beginning of the poem, the speaker's determination is expressed.' **(EVIDENCE)** 'This is achieved through the words: 'Better off dead than giving in'. **(EXPLORATION)**. The use of 'dead' emphasises how far the speaker is prepared to go in pursuit of what he wants, although there is a sense that he is exaggerating (hyperbole). **(EFFECT)** The listener senses that the speaker may be immature given how prone he is to exaggerate his own bravery.

STEP SIX: After writing five or more paragraphs like the one above, it will be time to write a **conclusion**. In order to do that, it is necessary to sum up your previous points and evaluate them. This is not the time to introduce additional quotations. Here is an example of what I mean: 'To conclude, the poet clearly conveys the speaker's anger. Although the listener will be reluctant to completely sympathise with a thief, there is a sense that the speaker is suffering mentally, which makes him an interesting and partially a sympathetic character. By using a dramatic monologue form, the poet effectively conveys the speaker's mental anguish, which makes it easier to more deeply understand what first appears to be inexplicable acts of violence.

Other tips

Make your studies active!

Don't just sit there reading! Never forget to annotate, annotate and annotate!

USEFUL INFORMATION (GLOSSARY)

Allegory: extended metaphor, like the grim reaper representing death, e.g. Scrooge symbolizing capitalism.

Alliteration: same consonant sound repeating, e.g. 'She sells sea shells'.

Allusion: reference to another text/person/place/event.

Ascending tricolon: sentence with three parts, each increasing in power, e.g. 'ringing, drumming, shouting'.

Aside: character speaking so some characters cannot hear what is being said. Sometimes, an aside is directly to the audience. It's a dramatic technique which reveals the character's inner thoughts and feelings.

Assonance: same vowel sounds repeating, e.g. 'Oh no, won't Joe go?'

Bathos: abrupt change from sublime to ridiculous for humorous effect.

Blank verse: lines of unrhymed iambic pentameter.

Compressed time: when the narrative is fast-forwarding through the action.

Descending tricolon: sentence with three parts, each decreasing in power, e.g. 'shouting, talking, whispering'.

Denouement: tying up loose ends, the resolution.

Diction: choice of words or vocabulary.

Didactic: used to describe literature designed to inform, instruct or pass on a moral message.

Dilated time: opposite compressed time, here the narrative is in slow motion.

Direct address: second person narrative, predominantly using the personal pronoun 'you'.

Dramatic action verb: manifests itself in physical action, e.g. I punched him in the face.

Dramatic irony: audience knows something that the character is unaware of.

Ellipsis: leaving out part of the story and allowing the reader to fill in the narrative gap.

End-stopped lines: poetic lines that end with punctuation.

Epistolary: letter or correspondence-driven narrative.

Flashback/Analepsis: going back in time to the past, interrupting the chronological sequence.

Flashforward/Prolepsis: going forward in time to the future, interrupting the chronological sequence.

Foreshadowing/Adumbrating: suggestion of plot developments that will occur later in the narrative.

Gothic: another strand of Romanticism, typically with a wild setting, a sensitive heroine, an older man with a 'piercing gaze', discontinuous structure, doppelgangers, guilt and the 'unspeakable' (according to Eve Kosofsky Sedgwick).

Hamartia: character flaw, leading to that character's downfall.

Hyperbole: exaggeration for effect.

Iambic pentameter: a line of ten syllables beginning with a lighter stress alternating with a heavier stress in its perfect form, which sounds like a heartbeat. The stress falls on the even syllables, numbers: 2, 4, 6, 8 and 10, e.g. 'When now I think you can behold such sights'.

Intertextuality: links to other literary texts.

Irony: amusing or cruel reversal of expected outcome or words meaning the opposite to their literal meaning.

Metafiction/Romantic irony: self-conscious exposure of the devices used to create 'the truth' within a work of fiction.

Motif: recurring image use of language or idea that connects the narrative together and creates a theme or mood, e.g. 'green light' in *The Great Gatsby*.

Oxymoron: contradictory terms combined, e.g. deafening silence.

Pastiche: imitation of another's work.

Pathetic fallacy: a form of personification whereby inanimate objects show human attributes, e.g. 'the sea smiled benignly'. The originator of the term, John Ruskin in 1856, used 'the cruel, crawling foam', from Kingsley's *The Sands of Dee*, as an example to clarify what he meant by the 'morbid' nature of pathetic fallacy.

Personification: concrete or abstract object made human, often simply achieved by using a capital letter or a personal pronoun, e.g. 'Nature', or describing a ship as 'she'.

Pun/Double entendre: a word with a double meaning, usually employed in witty wordplay but not always.

Retrospective: account of events after they have occurred.

Romanticism: genre celebrating the power of imagination, spriritualism and nature.

Semantic/lexical field: related words about a single concept, e.g. king, queen and prince are all concerned with royalty.

Soliloquy: character thinks aloud, but is not heard by other characters (unlike in a monologue) giving the audience access to inner thoughts and feelings.

Style: choice of language, form and structure, and effects produced.

Synecdoche: one part of something referring to the whole, e.g. Carker's teeth represent him in *Dombey and Son*.

Syntax: the way words and sentences are placed together.

Tetracolon climax: sentence with four parts, culminating with the last part, e.g. 'I have nothing to offer but blood, toil, tears, and sweat' (Winston Churchill).

ABOUT THE AUTHOR

Joe Broadfoot is a secondary head of English and a soccer journalist, who also writes fiction and literary criticism. His former experiences as a DJ took him to far-flung places such as Tokyo, Kobe, Beijing, Hong Kong, Jakarta, Cairo, Dubai, Cannes, Oslo, Bergen and Bodo. He is now PGCE and CELTA-qualified with QTS, a first-class honours degree in Literature and an MA in Victorian Studies (majoring in Charles Dickens). Drama is close to his heart as he acted in 'Macbeth' and 'A Midsummer Night's Dream' at the Royal Northern College of Music in Manchester. More recently, he has been teaching 'Much Ado About Nothing' and directing various Shakespearean plays.

Printed in Great
Britain
by Amazon